Swallow's Nest

Poetry Journal
of

OREGON CHRISTIAN WRITERS

Third Annual Issue — December 2021

Linda L. Kruschke, Editor-in-Chief
Sue Miholer, Copyeditor

Swallow's Nest published by Oregon Christian Writers

Linda L. Kruschke, Editor-in-Chief
Sue Miholer, Copyeditor

© 2021 by Oregon Christian Writers

All poets retain the copyright to their individual poems included in this journal.

ISBN: 9798759105459

Printed by Amazon KDP, An Amazon.com Company.
Available from Amazon.com and other retail outlets.

For Jesus, our Savior

Table of Contents

Preface

About *Swallow's Nest*

In 2019, Mary McIntosh and Rachel Lulich had the splendid idea to start an OCW poetry journal. Mary gave it the name *Swallow's Nest* based on a favorite verse in Psalm 84. I was honored to have my work included in the pages of the inaugural edition and to be asked to provide layout and design for that issue.

In 2020, I offered to once again do layout and design, and also to serve as the primary editor, and a tradition began.

For this third annual issue of *Swallow's Nest*, poets were allowed to submit up to three poems in the categories of Christmas, a New Year, or God's Creation. Initially I thought I would only choose one per poet but ultimately decided to include them all, organized by category.

Linda L. Kruschke
Editor-in-Chief

About Oregon Christian Writers

Founded in 1963, Oregon Christian Writers is an organization of writers, both amateur and professional, who are Christians. Our members write for both ministry and markets, and subscribe to a Statement of Faith based on the Apostles' Creed. Our aim is to glorify God and to help writers grow in their craft. OCW does not necessarily endorse the theological opinions expressed by its poets in these pages.

Christmas

Signs of the Season

~ Susan Brehmer

Busy, harried
Frenzy, flurry
All the season's
Obligations

Festive, merry
All together
Joyful hospitality

In the middle
Of the chaos
Christmas comes
In celebration

Tree lights sparkling
Candles glowing
Welcome signs
Of hearth and home

Are You Ready for Advent?

~ Tabitha B C Abel

No shrill, red-lighted ride along sleek paved streets,
   But the steady roll and plod of a donkey's feet
Lurching o'er rocks and through gullies.
In a virgin teen, with no prenatal care, chosen by God,
   the Christ-child to bear —

Not in a sanitized, shiny, delivery suite, But in a cold
   farm stall 'midst smelly chickens, cows and sheep.
With one long, final push and deafening yell, A tiny,
   wrinkled-faced nipper was squeezed out and fell
Into scratchy straw. He drew a breath — by God sent,
   thus Jesus was born on that First Advent!

The sound of clattering hooves and bells wafted
   through the air as Santa shouted "Ho, ho!"
Had Santa visited him this year?
Feverish fingers tore at crackling paper and glitzy
   ribbon, Revealing sugared mice, an orange — and
   chocolate coins to snack on.
Toy cars, a slinky, a beanie and a ball, and yes — a
   shiny spy-glass. He let out an excited cry, "I can't
   believe it's Christmas!"

The Nipper grew up. His mission misunderstood.
   Deserted — He was crucified.
The boy lost hope in a masked world of conspiracies,
   pretense and lies.

But a few heard the Lone voice saying "Follow Me.
    I'll give you peace
Amidst war, hate and pain, fear, death, loneliness,
    chaos, and injustice.
I am Faithful and True. I died for you and I *will* come
    again."
Could the man trust those words in his woebegone
    state and emotional pain?

He believed the Lone voice's words and gave Christ
    his messy life — a life far spent.
He believed the Words were true and rejoiced — then
    made ready for the Second Advent!

Are you ready?

Presence

~ Beryl Carpenter

In blue-fringed December
when winter freeze-dries
all living green to
shapes in steel wool

Then the flame of Christmas
traditions I would keep
heats my resolve to molten red
and quickens all my steps.

I hurry in a fever to do more
get more, be more
till all keeping of the season
leaves me spent — then

He comes quickly as
the sudden, silent snow
blankets all my harried plans
with alarm and fresh delight
and whispers

Do only this —
come as a child
celebrate my birthday
simply with me.

Jesus, King of Heaven

~ Laura Davis

See Him in the manger laid, Jesus, King of Heaven;
He, Who blood for sin would trade, Jesus, King of
    Heaven.
Innocent, our Prince of Peace gave His life to set us free.
Thank Him now on bended knee, Jesus, King of Heaven.

Mary, holding God's own Son, Jesus, King of Heaven,
Marveled at the Promised One, Jesus, King of Heaven.
Knowing not what trials would come, Joyful in what
    God had done,
Mother's love had just begun. Jesus, King of Heaven.

Long, the trail to Calvary for Jesus, King of Heaven,
Where His passion all would see. Jesus, King of Heaven.
How could promise turn to death, Change our fate with
    dying breath,
All alone complete His quest? Jesus, King of Heaven.

Then, on dawn's bright wings He came, Jesus, King of
    Heaven,
Conqu'ring with Messiah's Name, Jesus, King of
    Heaven.
Ris'n for all, the Lord of Hosts sends to earth the Holy
    Ghost,
Dearest Friend who loves us most — Jesus, King of
    Heaven.

Ramblings
of an Angel
in Disguise

~ Dorothy Doede

I remember Christmas
a long time ago
a long, long time ago

It was dark
then it wasn't
The morning stars sang for joy

like at the
Beginning
of the Story
only it wasn't the Beginning
it was the Middle

the Story with the Happy Ending

"The happy ending
cannot come
in the
middle
of the story."

Because that's the way it's written.

"In the beginning was the Word"
but that's the ending, too,
the Final Word

the Happy Ending
to the Story
that has
Christmas
in the
Middle.

Written as lines in a Christmas sketch for an
angel disguised as a bag lady mumbling into the
microphone at a church.

Remembering Christmas

~Sherri Langton

Winter feelings come as they please.
In them one remembers
the whipped white of deep freeze Decembers
and shimmering garland on Christmas trees;
pumpkin pie and fruit cake smells,
writing to Santa and "Jingle Bells";
wafer-thin frost on windowpanes
and barber pole stripes on candy canes;
dinners with family and slippery drives
through scenes print-perfect for Currier and Ives;
caroling and crunching through drifts of snow
that harden like candy at seven below.

But more than tastes and smells,
sounds and the glow,
is the One to remember
and to know His truth,
though ancient, is still gospel-fresh:
that the Light split darkness
and the Word became flesh.

Comfort and Joy

~ Lilia Salazar, Ph.D.

Would You wrap me in Your Arms
when I feel so alone in the quiet
of the night?

Would You touch me with Your warm
presence when my world seems
so cold?

Would You dry my tears flowing
freely when memories are all
that I have left?

Would You soothe my soul with hope
when I look at my bleak future with
despair and fear?

You are Immanuel.
God is with us.
God is with me.

You are bigger and stronger than any
of my sorrows.

You will never leave me, forsake me
nor abandon me.

You will assure me with victory over
all my deepest fears.

You will comfort me in my loneliness
as You prepare me for joy.

Tidings of comfort and joy;
I receive Your gift, oh Lord.
You're all I want for Christmas.

What Mystery?

~ Debbie Goodwin

What mystery was this

When Jesus came and how??

Transported through the air

From heaven's care?

How in a molecule,

No smaller still.

What atom did divinity fill and how

In woman planted?

How introduced?

How joined as whole?

I know the why

But at the how

I bow.

Why Shepherds

~ Robin Illers

Why were shepherds
the first invited guests
to see Jesus?
Why not the rest?

The innkeeper was busy
with his nightly chores,
turning away others
wanting through his doors.

Old friends remembered
times long gone by
all celebrating
till sunrise on high

Shepherds outside
guarding their sheep
vigilantly waiting
their charge they did keep.

Shepherds were watching
their flocks that night.
Still and listening.
They saw such a sight.

Angels from heaven
announced Jesus' birth:
The Son of God
come to live on earth.

Shepherds' Delight
(Luke 2:8–20)

~ Robin Illers

An angel appeared to shepherds
Announcing the Savior's birth:
God's plan of redemption
Come to dwell on earth.

"Fear not," the angel consoled them
"I bring you good news of great joy.
A child is born in Bethlehem,
Most precious baby boy.

He's the long-awaited Messiah.
The Prince of Peace is He.
God Himself, Emmanuel
Come to set captives free.

Follow the star and adore Him
Laid in a manger bare;
Swaddling cloths embrace Him,
The Christ Child, oh so fair."

The shepherds eagerly sought Him
Found just as the angel foretold,
Encouraged Mary and Joseph
With words from the angel bold.

Mary embraced the message
Sent by the angel above.
The shepherds returned with praises
Rejoicing in God's bundle of love.

My Christmas Eve

~ Charlotte Kardokus

Snow crunches underfoot
Icicles drip, snowballs bring revenge
Wind whistles thru barren oaks.

Smoke slithers above chimney tops
Darkness falls, stars twinkle
A familiar shout calls me in.

Mama's stew is scrumptious
But in the oven, a fruitcake. Ugh.
I prefer a candy cane.

We siblings sit, paper chains in hands
Silently gaze at mistletoe and stockings
Where did Mama and Daddy go?

Sounds emanate from closed door
Occasional laughter and frustration echoes
Was that a naughty word?

Mama and Daddy appear with
Fancy boxes, curly ribbons, bright bows
Is the biggest one mine?

A tall evergreen fills the corner
Angel atop, shiny bulbs, tinsel shimmering
Surprises wait beneath.

Eyes wide with wonder
Tummies and hearts filled with food and love
Off to bed, Mama says.

But before sleep, a story
Not a fairy tale, but words of a child born
In a stable, not a castle.

The best gift ever given
Jesus, our Savior, our gift from God
Don't ever forget.

Angel Messenger

~ Ginger Kauffman

Shining angel, majestic messenger from God,
what happened in Heaven
the day of the First Sin?
Did you and all the angels of God,
you who do His bidding,
gasp in disbelief
as you watched the seed of doubt,
cunningly planted,
take root and blossom into
disobedience?
Did you weep for all that was lost that day —
and all that was found?

Oh, the pain you have observed
from your Heavenly perspective,
the chaos,
the brokenness.
Did you know that God was working out a plan?
Were there whispers in Heaven?

Today he sends you to shepherds
with a message for the world:
"A Savior has been born!
Find a baby in a manger,
God's Son,
Christ the Lord!"

No wonder the angels of Heaven
burst into song!
"Glory to God!
Glory to God!
The Peace of Heaven has arrived!"

Old Zechariah

~ Ginger Kauffman

Old, you were old, Zechariah,
you and Elizabeth,
too old to have your prayer answered,
too old to have a child.

But your prayer was heard, Zechariah.
"A baby," the angel said,
"a son."

Dumbfounded, you were dumbfounded, Zechariah.
"How can I know for sure?" you asked.
Wrong question, Zechariah.

Dumb, you were struck dumb, Zechariah.
dumbstruck, nine months silent.

You were humble-struck by the one who struck you
        dumb.

When you held your son —
"John," you wrote, "his name is John" —
your tongue was loosed.

Awe-struck, you were awe-struck, old Zechariah,
father of the promised child,
in awe of the promise maker,
in awe of the promise keeper.

Filled, you were filled, Zechariah,
filled with God's Spirit,
filled with His praise
filled with His truth.

Old Zechariah, dumb-struck, humble-struck, awe-
        struck Zechariah,
tongue-loosed, praise-singing Zechariah.

Peace

~ Yvonne Kays

Where is the peace the angels proclaimed?

The earth still swirls with sin and pain.

Only humble hearts swept clean

Contain the Holy Gift.

Believe, trust, bow low.

Wise men still seek

Him to know.

Our true

Peace.

"Peace I leave with you, my peace I give you. I
do not give to you as the world gives. Do not let
your hearts be troubled and do not be afraid."
John 14:27 (NIV)

Previously published in *Bible Advocate*, July–
August 2020.

Once Upon a Time

~ Linda L. Kruschke

Once upon a starry night
A single star shown ever-bright
Outshone angels hovering a field
Telling shepherds who rightly kneeled
Of the birth of the Chosen One
Born of Mary, God's own Son

Wise men followed that singular star
Traveling for days from afar
With the shepherds they came to see
The King of kings who sets us free
Lying in a lowly manger stall
To save the lost, one and all

Each December I search the sky
But perhaps I should look in mid-July
Since we don't know when He was born
Was snow on the ground or fields full of corn
But the fact of His birth is true and sure
Faith in His grace will salvation secure

As we gaze upon a starry night
Let us not feud, bicker, and fight
May we prove hate is defeated by love
As we ponder the heavens above
Knowing we are never alone
And mercy sits upon His throne

Good News

~ Rachel Lulich

The Christmas hymns have all been sung;
The presents are under the tree,
Reminding us that wise men gave
Their gifts on bended knee.

"Fear not," the angel said, and told
The shepherds in the night,
That Christ was born in Bethlehem
To set the world aright.

So God was laid in a manger,
Made low for all to see.
He lived to die on a wretched cross
To make the sinner free.

And now, ascended in glory,
Forgiving our endless sin,
The Lord of all will return one day,
And all will worship him.

Previously published in *To Do This Right: Poems of Faith* (2018).

Simply Wrapped

~ Maxine Marsolini

O' Christmas tree of fragrant boughs
Bejeweled with twinkling lights
Lure hearts and eyes beyond your spell
To see Christ's love — simply wrapped

O' brilliant star in winter sky
Attract all curious trekkers
To see the light of God's best gift
Dear Christmas Child's redeeming peace

Countdown to Christmas

~ Sue Miholer

'Twas days before Christmas, and all through the house
The wife was a'running, reminding her spouse:

"You have to shop for your folks this year;
I don't have the time to do it, my dear.
Your father likes tools; your mother likes pink.
Last year we gave them . . . sweaters, I think.

"And, yes, we're going to the program at school.
I know it's boring, dear, but try to stay cool.
Of course it's true that our kids sing offkey,
But they certainly didn't get that from me!

"I don't see how I'll get all the baking done.
Let's try doing it together. Wouldn't that be fun?
You and the kids can make gingerbread men
While I make Grandmother's fruitcake again.

"I took all our cards to the mailbox today
And am glad that project's out of the way!
I addressed one to every name on our list,
But I just know there's someone I missed.

"Anne is in charge of the program at church.
She called today to say she'd be left in the lurch
If she didn't find someone to be Joseph this year.
I told her you'd do it. OK, my dear?

"The dollhouse for Megan will look really nice
If you follow the sheet that gives you advice.
And instructions for Aaron's new bike firmly state
That all of the parts are included — isn't that great?

"Have you seen their wish lists to Santa this year?
We can't afford a one of their dream toys, I fear.
Of course, each thing cleverly designed to please
Requires investing in a caseload of batteries.

"There's a robot that's programmed to totter about.
(Perhaps we could train it to let the dog out.)
There are dollies and bears in every shape and size —
Even some that can wink their eyes.
And there are tractors and trains and cars and trucks.
Believe me, all of them cost plenty of bucks!

"I tried to finish my shopping today
When I went to the mall with Brenda and Kay.
I felt like a rat that was running a maze.
I came out of there with my mind in a haze.

"Shopping this year is really a pain.
I shopped all day — and what did I gain?
Two feet that are sore, more credit card bills,
A tension headache and stomach ills."

With a sigh and a groan she sank into her chair,
In hopes that the new year soon would be there.
"Next year will be different," she quietly mused,
As into a nap she wistfully snoozed.

If Christ Had Not Come

~ Ava Pickard

When we come to this blessed time of the year
To praise the birth of God's Son
I can't help but ponder our certain doomed fate
If Jesus, our Lord, had not come —
If He had not come to the manger that night
Two thousand and some years ago —
The star in the east would never have shown
To herald His birth down below.
The wise men would never have carried the gold,
Their myrrh and frankincense shared —
The shepherds could never have followed that star
To the birthplace that God had prepared.
And Jesus Himself would never have touched
All those lost and dying on earth . . .
To give such a gift to all who would come
And began with His very own birth
The blind man who saw after washing himself
From the clay Christ placed on his eyes —
Would never have caught even one glimpse of light
From the rays that shown from the skies . . .
The widow that passed on the street where He walked,
And mourning the death of her son —
Would never have seen the glory of God
When Jesus cried, "Death — be done!"

So many, yes millions of lives that have known
The touch of His wonderful grace
Would never have heard the sound of His voice
Or felt His loving embrace!
If Jesus had stayed where He felt so secure,
Had not left His heavenly home —
I wonder, myself, just where would I be
If my Savior and Lord had not come?

Simeon's Messiah

~ Terri Picone

Simeon believed
When the Holy Spirit promised him:
Before he died,
The Messiah he would see.

The One to restore Israel,
The Savior of the whole world,
For all who would see His light,
He was coming.
Simeon believed.

In the temple complex,
He waited for that day
And Anna, too, a prophetess,
Waiting, watching, waiting . . .

And that day
Joseph and Mary bring Jesus
To the temple,
as required by law,
(His coming fulfills the law),
Bringing also their sacrifice
To redeem their firstborn
(Who came to redeem us all).

The crowds,
dispersed throughout the temple complex,
Worship and barter;
lambs bleat, doves coo.

And the sweet aroma of burnt sacrifices —
Grain offerings and meat offerings —
The earthy, musky smells of anointing oil
And the cry of the Baby Savior
Fill Joseph and Mary with wonder,
They are filled with wonder,
When the Holy Spirit reveals a sign:
This is the very One promised to our fathers.
He will expose, reveal, pierce hearts
He is our Redeemer.

Departing through the crowded temple,
Simeon's song, Anna's prayers echo behind them.
Joseph and Mary slip into the marketplace beyond,
toward home,
And Mary ponders their words.

Will you believe like Simeon and Anna
Like Joseph and Mary?
Will you rend your heart
And see Him?

He is coming again.
It is promised.
He is coming again.
It is certain.
He is coming again.
Will you see Him?

Snow Waltz

~ Kathleen R. Ruckman

A wintry waltz debuts today,
Shimmering ballroom on display.
Swirls and twirls cascading down,
Snowflakes dancing 'round the town.

Fragrant pines all clothed in white,
Scarlet cardinal, God's delight.
Image of redeeming glory,
Red and white, a holy story.

Fluffy flakes fall on my nose.
Icy temps scrunch up my toes.
Waltzing snowflakes warm my heart,
Each unique—a work of art.

Looking upward in a trance,
I hear the silence of this dance.
Crystal gems designed with grace,
In triple time spin into place.

Farther than my eyes can see,
Waltzing flakes fall soft on me.
Before the flurries touch the earth,
Untainted symbol, my new birth.

Whisked away in joyful swing,
Winter's cold turns into spring.
A gift from God, this holy lace,
That I may see Him face to face.

"Purge me with hyssop, and I shall be clean;
Wash me, and I shall be whiter than snow."
Psalm 51:7 (NKJV)

Royal Manger

~ Katheen R. Ruckman

A place for God, a crib of hay,
Bleating sheep and a donkey's bray.
Unlikely home for Majesty,
A humble, royal pageantry.

If I had journeyed to this place,
I might have knelt to kiss His face,
Where destiny would press a thorn,
Where Peace personified was born.

The King of Heaven came to die,
God's love within a Baby's cry.
Eternal life, wrapped in glory,
With sovereign pen God wrote His story.

Redeeming love from Christ came down,
Cradle, cross, and lasting crown.
Suffering servant, Man of Sorrows,
Hope and joy for my tomorrows.

The bells of Christmas toll for me,
Resounding through eternity.
God knows my name and I'm no stranger.
I am welcome at the manger.

"To God our Savior,
Who alone is wise,
Be glory and majesty,
Dominion and power,
Both now and forever.
Amen."
Jude 1:25 (NKJV)

Christmas Rose

~ Kathleen R. Ruckman

Like summer roses in full bloom,
A fragrance fills the stable room.
Bleating sheep and Baby's cry,
Blend in with a mother's sigh.

With joy to hold the Savior near,
His mother tastes a salty tear.
Her fingers gently trace His face,
Where thorns one day would take their place.

Holy garden, straw, and cold
Unfold the mystery as foretold.
Heaven's Blossom fills the stall,
Hope for the world in One so small.

Hosts of angels hover high,
Holy hush in sacred sky.
The Great Exchange: my sin, His grace,
Sweet Lamb of God to take my place.

Petals crushed on Calvary,
The essence trickles down for me.
Rising incense, Love made known,
Eternal Flower — Christ alone.

"Walk in the way of love, just as Christ loved us and gave
himself up for us as a fragrant offering and sacrifice to God."
Ephesians 5:2 (NIV)

A New Year

The Best-Ever New Year

~ Tabitha B C Abel

New plans. New me. New hope. New Year!
Forget the loss 'n pain, the insanity and drear.
Roll out the old, roll in the new!
But will it stick and make the old you new?

Change takes more effort than changing just one
    digit,
You can't self-remodel by adjusting just one
    widget.
It takes a re-Creator to style a lasting makeover,
So invite Him to walk right in and take you
    over.

Give Him your time and money, your temper
    and will,
Your harsh words and white lies — and swallow
    the pill!
Wipe the slate clean and give him the lot —
He'll re-create beauty from a dumpster of rot.

"Lord, create in me a clean heart and put a right
    spirit in me,
Make me willing to be molded into what You'll
    have me be.
Let me be kind to all, teach truth and Your love
    share.
Re-create me, O Lord, and make this the best-
    ever New Year!"

Perspective

~ Susan Brehmer

Stepping forward
Looking back

A glimpse ahead
A glance behind

Thankful to forge ahead
Grateful for what's been learned

A distant view
Whether on the horizon
Or in the rearview mirror

Appears small from far away
But grows as we focus
And move toward it

Which direction will you look?

Midnight's Choice

~ Chara Donahue

I must make the choice. It's on me.
What to believe? What to negate?
Tonight I ask, which voice will it be?

Live in the light determined to see,
or let depravity poison future's fate?
I must make the choice. It's on me.

Passively cower? An internal absentee?
Will truth employed set lies straight?
Tonight I ask, which voice will it be?

Declaring by the midnight hour is key.
What will my time communicate?
I must make the choice. It's on me.

Resist and make dark thoughts flee.
Leave behind these chains, this weight.
Again I asked, which voice would it be?

From accusation and doubt, an escapee.
With mind renewed I celebrate.
I will make the choice to live; be free.
This year I declare: God's voice it will be!

Cup of New

~ Amy Earls

I don't want to remember old acquaintance.
I don't want to remember when we took a cup of
      kindness because we didn't have masks in the
      way.
I don't want to think that happiness is when you
      remove your mask and shock yourself with a
      smile in the reflection of your mirror.
Because the truth is,
your smile will be tired,
Zoomed-out.

I recall when I wasn't tired. It was a season to rest and
      drink kindness, to be happy in the new.

Years.
They're seasonal.
Like summer to winter with no transition in between.
Like a half-full, half-empty glass.

Next time you see yourself in the mirror, I want you
      to tell yourself,

I know what you have seen with your unmasked
      eyes.
I know how you have grieved for your neighbors,
      family, and country.
I know the winter season hasn't ended.

But I want you to remind yourself

that God is just so dang good
that He's taken off His mask—has torn the curtain
        between us and Him—
to raise a cup and say,
"Cheers to our friendship. Cheers to My kindness.
        Cheers to My love for you."

Years.
New.
Happy.
Remember.

Sleep Well

~ Gail Denham

My
middle
feels relief
as God removes
fear, spreads salve on hurts.
His hand grasps mine tight, while
effervescence sweeps through. God
takes the night watch so that I can
sleep. When I wake, joy surges, burbles
up from my toes, spreads peace through my body.

King of Glory

~ Linda Heath

King of Glory
through ancient gates
White horse stamping
ready to charge
Lord of Victory
Faithful and True
Rides into battle
The Breaker goes out
He leads us through
Bursts through the barriers
Freedom's charge
Wake up Ancient Gates
To the Mighty One
Give welcome to your King
You, yes you
His gateway to ride through
For battles won and victory secure
Praise to our King of Glory
Armed in Splendor
Victorious One
Riding in holiness
We bow in awe
Offering up all praise
To the only
Worthy
King of Glory

untitled

~ Tracie Heskett

new beginnings,
new day, new week, new year,
return from vacation—
an opportunity
to slide back into routines
an old pair of jeans,
a comfortable blanket.

a mug of warm creamy cocoa,
blue spiral prayer notebook,
Bible with front cover torn loose
pear tree out the window
home—my soothing place,
knowing significant other will walk
in that evening.

I fold my routines
around me
structure gives freedom

My New Year

~ Charlotte Kardokus

Hours stuck behind a desk,
Dreams of free time and more rest.
Did I hear retirement's fun?
But not always right for everyone?

No set time I must arrive,
No constraint to work 'til five.
No more bennies, no more pay,
Dare I go or should I stay?

Mind awhirl, I must choose,
Either way, I cannot lose.
With options flirting, I can be free,
Eyes wide open, yet I cannot see.

Choice is made; it's time to leave.
Shall I dance, or should I grieve?
Plans are blurred for days ahead,
I try to smile, but yet I dread.

Prayers are sent, all things in order,
As I skirt this unknown border.
Faith, without doubt, devoid of fear,
Must be the key for my new year.

Morning Song

~ Ginger Kauffman

The day is fresh and new.
Rose scent fills the air,
the house ticks like an old clock shop.

I sit by the window
sipping tea,
absorbing the quietness,
listening to robins hunting worms
in the yard.

When was my heart last still?
When was my mind last able to see the world?
When was my body last rested?

I release the breath I've been holding for days,
I drop my hands to my sides.
I hear the words,
"Come to me, weary one."
Ready now, I come.

Clean Slate

~ Maxine Marsolini

A quick turn of the calendar page
At toll of midnight bells
We part company with what once was
Imagine what can be
Clean slate of days to write

Such a fresh reminder of God's grace
That buries past regrets
Beside self-reproach and awkward shame
Beneath the ocean's depths
Clean slate of life to live

A New Year, A New Day

~ Terri Picone

A new year means a new day,
A renewed day, a second chance.
Why are we so hard-hearted,
Wanting our own way, insisting on our own thing?

Yet God gives us what we want,
Lets us run away.

It's only through His grace to us
That we finally see our folly,
Rend our hearts and turn back.

And He gives us a second chance,
Yes, another chance, a new day!
It's a new year.
Starting today.

God's Creation

Thank You

~ Dorothy Doede

Thank You, Father God,
for choosing writing
to reflect Your artistic creativity
in me.

I like the flow of words
swirling from my mind
cascading out my fingers
coursing down the page
to pool for reflection

I like time for
choosing words
crafting sentences
building paragraphs
to fling together a frame

I like leisure in
thinking things through
editing and rewriting
formatting and arranging
to scrawl in pen and ink

I like this craft of unhampered precision.

Thank You, Jesus,
for choosing writing
for me.

A Snowy Day

~ Dorothy Doede

The sun peeks out
tiptoeing into the blue layer
sandwiched between
frilly cafe curtain clouds.

The falling snow took its cue
and left the stage,
content in knowing
its quietly dramatic performance
was of the highest caliber,
the set gloriously changed
by its soft presence.

The valley is white now
as are the hills.
The trees stand tall
modeling their new thick coats —
white on green.

It is peaceful and still —
no wind
no cars
Only creation willingly performing
for its Creator
and His guests.

Dark gray-whiteness spreads,
        obscuring much of the valley.
A hint of pink traces the outline
        of snow-painted branches
        to mark where the sun retired.

The new fallen snow covers the tracks
        of bold adventurers —
        explorers of a brave new world.

Darkness will come
        drawing the curtain on

        "A Snowy Day
            in March
            in Oregon."

Glorious Possibility

~ Beryl Carpenter

We live by algorithms
Patterns regular, comforting
Sometimes cruel

Rhythm of the spheres
Stark winter follows summer in
All its excess

Flowers and fruit
Sun and shade
Dry grass igniting

Gnarled branches
Shedding summer coats
An icy hand, sudden snow

Stars parade the sky
In perfect cadence
We age and limp away

Solomon knew
A time for everything
Life's joy and regret

We intend
Never to follow through
Spirit willing, flesh weak

God breaks through
Defying formulas
Radical invader

Restoring the broken
Redeeming the crushed
Renewing possibility

Grace asserts
Its gentle anarchy
Silent splendor

Song of My Heart

~ Shirley Dechaine

You are the song of my heart, my love
And these words are penned for you
Your love is a gift from our Father above
A blessing beyond compare.

Ten years have passed since first we met
And in these years we have grown
Turning away from old ways that build walls and
     keep us apart
Our souls unite, bringing ever-increasing tenderness.

In the year I met you, dear, my heart was sadly torn
I knew I had lost my way
The light of your friendship opened the door
Can I express what that means today?

Over the years that we've been together
I've seen the sunshine more than the grey
Your smiling eyes, the warmth of your love
Have truly brought gladness along my way.

This is my song for you, my love
The way I choose to express
A deep settled happiness founded in His peace
Extended in your companionship
Because you open yourself up to me
And let me share your life.

For all these reasons and so many more, I love you!

Written by Shirley Dechaine for her husband,
Don, on their tenth wedding anniversary.

He Is Our Creator

~ Tabitha B C Abel

Down on their knees, beneath songbirds in trees,
From dust, God sculpted both Adam and Eve
  —not Adam and Steve.
God brought them to life, and wed the man to his
  wife,
Saying, "Go populate the earth in My image."

Then came God's bless'd day. The last act of
  creation
The Sabbath, for peoples of ev'ry nation,
His sacred, chosen day, with Him to sing and pray,
Awed by His goodness and blessings ev'ry day.
Our Creator's gift.

But we ignore our Creator and do our own thing.
Marry who we will and have our little fling—
We forget to meet with God on His sacred day.
Ignoring His call because we want our own way.
We are ungrateful.

But time is running out. Read His Word—you'll
    understand.
Don't let the Devil hoodwink you and ignore
    salvation's plan.
He is the Creator of the universe and every living
    creature, rock and tree.
So let us keep God's day holy and only to Him
    bend our knee—
For He is Our Creator.

Is It Warm in Heaven?

~ Gail Denham

My friend and I are much closer to heaven
now than those teen years when we tore
around town in flats with no sox in the snow,
refused to wear jackets.

Is it warm in heaven? We won't need the seven
cords of wood — all those tractor loads husband
gathered, chopping dead trees, splitting firewood.

Sunday, I wore two layers of clothing. Some
meeting halls, like our small church, chill
to the bone by time Pastor says the "amen."

Will we be warm in that future place? Can't have
wood smoke coat those golden streets with ash,
spread a film on our mansion windows.

The temperature will be perfect, controlled by our
Savior who has it all ready. No need to adjust furnace
settings, like when husband's gone, and I'm too tired
to build a fire, and he's got that blasted thermostat
automatically set at "ECO." Don't ask.

Origin

~ Amy Earls

At the end of the trail,
at the rim of the water,
I see the exceptional,

the Divine's fingerprint in each delicate lily.

I step into the marsh,
dig my toes into the muddy waters,
and sink until the water reaches my calves.

The sun covers my face.
I am warm here.

I stay.
Rooted.
Planted, like a tree.

This is what I was created for.
To be grafted with Creator.
To resemble my Father.

Oh, great Maker,
how can I not fall on my knees and
worship from such splendor —
the tree of life,
the bird's song full of praise,
the reed that dances in the breeze.

Breathing Faith

~ Chara Donahue

Sacred romance embrace my heart. Desire
ignite the flame. No fear of being hurt.
A love affair, silent and bare. Inhale
to stand alive. I run to play with fire.
Untamed, so wild, the danger tempts, I come
to You. Oh, Lord, embrace my spirit, I'll taste
the life You died to give. I will not waste
the zest, the zeal. I breathe, no longer numb.

The thunderstorm, the lightning chase, vibrant
I pace the pulse of joy. Exhale in shouts,
In praise, I sing. To learn I want it all.
To turn away is sin. I won't; I can't.
Resound the heart of God, with faith, not doubt,
Not safe, but worth the risk. Answer the call.

The Rock

~ Sharon Chase Hoseley

It's happened again, hasn't it? The heart has been
crushed. The person you've trusted most has pushed
the delete button leaving you empty and lost, a no-
body. It seemed secure to trust in the presence of this
human being. It's easy to forget that life is limited to
emotions,
Flaws, imperfection and
Instability without Jesus.

There's no person solid, stable or strong enough.
There's no perfect peace.
There's no complete trust.
Except in . . .

JESUS—"the Only Rock" in this "lost in space" time
of abandonment.
He's the solid, stable strength you long for.
He's the peace under all circumstances.
He's the dependable one, always there.
Leap into His waiting arms and be found.

"You protect me with salvation-armor; you hold me up with a
firm hand, caress me with your gentle ways. You cleared the
ground under me so my footing was firm."
Psalm 18:32–36 (MSG)

Previously published in *Jesus, Lord of My
Season's—Hard Places* (2007).

Scattered Diamonds

~ Debbie Goodwin

Scattered diamonds on the water,
Shimmer-stones of magic light.
    Try to capture
    Cannot touch them
They are only yours by sight.

Lightning bugs, a dance unfolding;
Beauty catchers must be bold,
    Do not tarry;
    They are treasures
Only for the heart to hold.

Glory Falls

~ Debbie Goodwin

The gold medallion drops and
Slips down the day's necklace
Suspended for seconds only.
But in the slow fall
Glory spreads
As gold
The day has not known.
Burning orange of glowing coal
Backwashed in peach.
This is how
Glory falls.

A Brumal Adventure

~ Mary A. Hake

Beautiful scenery—the journey is fine,
Skillful maneuvering, hemlock to pine.

Mountains crisscrossing rise into view;
Nature's vast presence shows itself true.

Snow-laden trees seem to struggle with life.
Railroads scar the landscape with strife.

A river flows placidly, nourishing the land;
Beside its calm waters regal elk stand.

Wildlife abounds in this wilderness haven,
Evidenced in snow by distinct tracks engraven.

Sunlight streams down from a brilliant blue sky;
Kaleidoscopic reflections bedazzle the eye.

The lake's frozen splendor is a snowman's delight,
With winter's white sentinels guarding the site.

Cold grips the air in a strangling hold,
Chilling and killing the venturous bold.

Darkness envelopes; the timid sun flees,
Enclosed in a tunnel formed from tall trees.

Pursued by the clouds, swallowed up in the night,
Silent solitude in a forest of fright.

Escape is uncertain—a treacherous path . . .
Beauty remains the aftermath.

In the Stillness

~ Linda Heath

I hold my breath.
The stillness captures me.
Quiet. Absorbing.
An all-encompassing pause.
Into this stillness
I hear
the whisper of feathers.
I see
Nothing there.
And yet,
a Presence.
I feel the glowing,
pulsating comfort and strength,
Surrounded,
filled with wonder,
I wait.
What are you saying to me, Lord?
In this stillness.
With this Presence.
And the brush of angel wings?
Comes the still small voice:
Loved.
Treasured.
Empowered.
Commissioned.
Hear My heart.
Go share My heart.
Love! Go!

Soaring

~ Linda Heath

Teetering on the edge
Untried wings outstretched
Falling into space
I fly

Up from underneath
Supporting and sustaining
I am not alone
I fly

Ruach Adonai
Breath beneath my wings
Lifting me above
I fly

Leaping off with joy
Gaining strength and speed
Hearing whispered Truth
I fly

Soaring to the heights
Effortlessly gliding
Above the noise of earth
I soar

A Hundred Billion

~ Helen Heavirland

A hundred billion . . .
If you counted one number
Every second for a hundred years,
You'd reach three billion,
One hundred fifty-five million,
Seven hundred sixty thousand.
To reach a hundred billion,
You'd have to count
One number every second
For three thousand, sixty-nine years.

A hundred billion . . .
The number of nerve cells*
God created in your brain
Keeping heart, lungs, and liver,
Lymph, eyes, and capillaries
Functioning. Keeping
Thought active
And sleep restorative.
A hundred billion nerve cells . . .
Fearfully and wonderfully made.

*Includes neurons and neuroglia.

God Spoke

~ Helen Heavirland

God spoke and there was
Light, air, dry land and sea,
There were lights in sky,
Creatures flying and swimming,
Beasts on earth.

God spoke through prophets
And plagues fell,
Fire burned offering and altar,
Pagans by thousands repented.

God in flesh spoke
And fishermen followed,
Muscles stretched and flexed,
Corpses breathed, walked, praised.

God spoke through common people —
Gospels were written. God speaks
Through work done well, a smile, a hand up,
And through words that pluck heartstrings
With chords that echo through eternity.

With

~ Tracie Heskett

words jabbed

my fragile balloon

wilted on the floor

I walked in pre-dawn stillness

words drifted through my mind

prayer fragments

to the One who hears

Darkness faded to day

a few words remembered

to write the Journey.

Unloosing

~ Tracie Heskett

you have to slow down
to see poetry
pulsing
leaping
erratic movements
like a child at play

you have to be quiet
to hear poetry
the rhythm of life
silence speaking
so loud
it cannot be ignored

you have to be still
to feel poetry
to write poetry
as it shapes you
into something
you've never been before

His Creation

~ Charlotte Kardokus

In memory of Annie 1952–2021

Her hand holds tightly to my arm,
As I lead her through the department store.
I glance, see her smile as we approach the snack bar.
She loves popped corn or French fries. And soda.

Her eyes twinkle but can't see fingers point,
Her freshly shampooed hair covers dulled ears.
I hear the comments, sometimes rude,
Perhaps spoken in ignorance, or maybe on purpose.

Born with dimmed sight and no hearing,
Glimpses of brightness soon disappeared.
Leaving a world of darkness, yet her soul shines,
God's creation, valuable as gold and silver.

An occasional burst of laughter, what is she thinking?
Her hands search for the popcorn bag and soda cup.
I hear murmurs coming from behind.
I turn, perhaps they'll understand if I explain.

"She's my sister," I offer with lips trembling.
"She's no different than you or me,"
I pause, watch curious eyes stare at her.
"It's not her fault she's deaf and blind."

I lead her to the exit door, to the street.
We walk sidewalks, rough and bumpy,
Carefully so she won't stumble or fall.
I must protect her, even if I'm bruised.

She sits in her rocking chair,
Book open, fingers moving over braille words.
"What is her world like?" I wonder.
What if our roles were reversed?

Would she care? Or abandon me,
If I lived with the challenges she's been given.
Handicapped, impaired, disabled,
All means the same in God's eyes.

He loves no person less than another.
For God so loved the world,
That He exchanged His life for ours.
All are as silver and gold in His eyes, regardless.

Witness

~ Julie Kepler

The mockingbird's name betrayed
the melodies I heard today.
He didn't mock the jay or lark,
but sang to the Creator's heart,
and leaped and hopped
from branch to branch
like David dancing before the ark.

Such gyrations for a bird
may seem a little bit absurd,
but people stopped and stared as he
sang with such sincerity.
A constant stream of sounds and psalms
tumbled from the treetop boughs
and spoke, to those below,
in tongues.

Oh, that I will spend my days
giving God such endless praise!

Previously published in *The Christian Journal*,
March 2005.

Invitation

~ Julie Kepler

On this startling, clear morning,
a cloudless azure sky
collides
with solid rock stretched high and wide.

Across the panoramic view,
Heaven pours down blessing —
crystal blue and crisp, fresh wind —
as if an invitation has ensued
to leave one's sins and follow Him.

Below, the mesa holds a stony stance —
its strangely straight horizon line
unyielding
to this winsome Heavenly advance.

Beneath its hard, unwavering edge,
resistant rimrock columns
rise. Side by side, silent ranks
like soldiers
buttress, bolster and uphold
the mesa's barren, flat plateau.

Perhaps this is a picture —
portrayed in nature's art —
of how it is when
Heaven's soft salvation call
falls on a hardened heart.

Emergence

~ Yvonne Kays

The Creator but spoke.
The world became reality.
He reveals deep and secret things
To those who have eyes to see.

I stare at the rock in my hand.
I draw a line, a dot;
Now with beak and eye,
A tiny hummingbird
Emerges.
Hovering erect, wings aflutter,
No longer hidden in flinty rock,
Unveiled for all to see.

I revel in the pleasure of creativity
ingrained in me,
A creature made in the image
of the
Most Creative One.

Better Than Magic

~ Linda L. Kruschke

It's in their DNA
to sip then zip away
Hovering in one spot
as other birds cannot

The agile hummingbird
Magical is the only word
That will adequately describe
members of this tribe

Even magic is not enough
To illuminate the Creator's
amazing stuff

In His Image Is Beauty

~ Linda L. Kruschke

In winter all stands bare and stark
Days fall short, nights bathed in dark
Snowflakes light on branches of trees
In this image beauty I see

Heather before spring does bloom
Chasing away winter's dark gloom
For warmth and more flowers my plea
In this image beauty I see

Crocus sprout next from cold ground
Spring has come when sunshine abounds
I smile to hear the buzzing bees
In this image beauty I see

Hummingbird calls my yard his home
Not far from nectar source to roam
Chasing rival he buzzes me
In this image beauty I see

Cooper's hawk soars high in the sky
Spying songbirds with his sharp eye
Though sometimes his lunch they will be
In this image beauty I see

Gray hair and wrinkles come with age
Life of man and beast turn a page
Death comes to all we must agree
In life's image beauty I see

For our sins He hung on the cross
Loved ones wept and mourned this great loss
Yet because of Him death does flee
In His image beauty I see

Behold creation and you'll know
Jesus is God from long ago
At His throne all will bend the knee
In His beauty we are set free

Daisies Tell

~ Grace Kyser

Fields of tall grasses were bursting with white-petalled daisies under the overcast Oregon summer sky.

He loves me, he loves me not.

The trail to Mt Baldy was cloaked in many colors: golden wheat, green grass, gray stones, brown dirt, deciduous and evergreen trees. But the flowers were commanding my attention on this day. A small drainage pond was draped with daisies as they peered into the dark waters below.

He loves me, he loves me not.

Hiking through the fields, I remembered Psalm 23, how the poet David wrote of the Good Shepherd leading him beside still waters to rest and restore his soul.

He loves me, he loves me not.

Among the thick blackberry bushes, two small plantings of wild daisies peeked through the high grasses with their bright white petals and golden centers, taunting me with

He loves me, he loves me not.

Who could question the beauty, the colors, the layering of nature—God's creation!

"For You created all things,
and by Your will they exist and
were created."
Revelation 4:11 (NKJV)

Yet being the gracious, generous God He is, He shares it with all the earth, not holding back anything from us.

He loves me, He loves me not.

Even Solomon in all his glory was not adorned like the flowers of the field. If that's how God clothes the grass of the field, which is here today and thrown into the furnace tomorrow, won't He do much more for you?
(*See* Matthew 6:29–30)

He loves me.

Woodpecker

~ Susan Thogerson Maas

Your tap-tap-tap
Echoes through the woods,
Draws me forward,
Slowly, quietly.
Where are you?
I search the trees,
Looking for movement.
Finally I spot you,
Pecking at a branch,
Wood chips flying.
Tap-tap-tap.
You stop to slurp up
The tiny insects.
Tap-tap-tap.
Do you know you weaken
The limb on which you perch?
Tap-tap-tap.
The branch bends beneath you.
You stop, wait, consider,
Then lift your wings and fly.
I turn back to the path,
Warmth touching my spirit,
Because I know
I, too, have been given wings.

God Did It Right

~ Michael Mailloux

Morning wakes to newborn day
Igniting nature's view.
Sunrise splendor on display
Enhancing springtime hue.

Sound of river's joyful cry
Through woods of evergreen.
Nightingales' sweet lullaby
Give voice to quiet scene.

Twilight brings a silent hush
Of calming heartfelt cheer.
Followed by late sunset blush
Night sky to soon appear.

Darkness puts the day to rest
As stars show their delight.
We have seen Him at His best
Yes, our God did it right.

God's Melody

~ Michael Mailloux

No greater song to orchestrate
With voices God did innovate.
Rustling leaves of windblown trees,
Chirping crickets, buzzing bees.

Shouts of thunder fill the sky,
Followed by the raindrops' cry.
Moments pause of silent still,
Gleaming light from rainbows thrill.

We hear, oh God, Your joyful rhyme
In singing birds and church bell chime.
From gentle stream to roaring sea
There is no greater melody.

God's Melody brings Tranquility

Season's Journey

~ Michael Mailloux

Brilliant hue of fall's display
Surrendering to winter's way.
Springtime and its whispered rhyme
Bring full voice to summertime.

From silent snow to robin's song,
Seasons journey on and on.
Take a moment; thank your guide,
Continue on with nature's ride.

Stillness

~ Sandy McCulloch

If you want to know Me,
    Rise early
Before the first glimmers
Of dawn soften the darkness.
Leave the downy warmth
Of your bed and tiptoe
    Outside.
Sit wrapped in fleecy silence,
Heart and breath slowed.
Listen and watch
As cobalt blackness fades
To cerulean
And gray shadows
Of familiar things
Emerge around you.

Then
    just before

    Star vanishes star,
    Avian song heralds the day,
Or   Wind ruffles the lake

I'll be there.

River

~ Terri Picone

The river meanders, rushes, and sometimes falls
Along the path set for it,
It brings its gifts and is, by its nature,
Life-sustaining.

A boundary between here and there.
A divider of states, countries, languages.
But, too, a conduit toward another place,
A connector to another river or a lake or an ocean.

A gift of wonder and awe, a glimpse of our Creator.
We are like a river. As we pass through life,
Though each distinct, we also connect to others
In ways that reflect our Creator, Giver of Life.

God's Evidence

~ Susan Wade

Let us wake up and step outside to see what this
day has to offer.

I'll walk for a change and not ride, a new memory I
want to go for.

Only God can make scenery like this, mountains in
the background, tall green trees all around.

Yet, right where I'm standing I see a bench for me
to go sit on.

There's a crystal-clear lake with some logs on the
side, young deer not making a sound.

I hear chipmunks and squirrels chipping away,
stopping to sit up and listen.

Jack rabbits are bouncing around as they play, dew
on the ground wet with glisten.

The atmosphere smells incredibly crisp with fall in
the air; it is damp.

I'm ever so grateful for the magnificence of Your
creation, every day is always a gift.

Today I want to make a memory with You, to relax
and talk a bit.

Message of Love

~ Susan M. Wade

When you were young you didn't notice how
much I truly cared.

But every day I followed you to watch how your
life fared.

I loved you when you couldn't tell, I saw when
you obeyed.

I softened out your steps for you even when you
strayed.

Today I've called you by your name; your sins are
all forgiven.

Stand firm in how you value things; be led by Me
not driven.

Listen very carefully as My words accomplish
much.

My truth will bring you lasting peace and others
you will touch.

Love Rules

~ Susan M. Wade

For too long I let the voice of hate taunt me in my
ear

Until I hollered, "Heaven help me rid myself of
fear."

It isn't what I want in life; I know it holds me back.

It paralyzes both my feet and makes my mouth
attack.

My mind starts thinking useless things, imagining
the worst

while my spirit begs for freedom that is blessed
without a curse.

Your word says love's a better way — that hope
must never part,

that once it's learned the fear will leave then love
will rule my heart.

Little One

~ Judy Williams

Little one, your time with us had not begun

You've never felt the warm, soft sun

Or walked on snow or touched a cat

Your time with us had not begun

Yet we love you, little one.

And we know, while now apart

You are safe and snug with God's own Son.

We let Him now, your Shepherd be

Until in heaven, you, we'll see!

About the Poets

Poet biographies are listed in reverse alphabetical order, by last name, just to mix things up. Those with last names beginning with *W* shouldn't always be at the end of the line. Call it poetic license on my part.

∞ ∞ ∞ ∞ ∞ ∞ ∞

When not traveling, **Judy Williams** chases her ten grandchildren, enjoys writing and doing crafts. She operates a Women's Ministry called Possibili-Teas at a local Christian camp. Judy loves God's Word and a good cup of tea.
(Page 101)

Currently **Susan M. Wade** is working part time driving troubled kids to school and back. Also, she is resurrecting her Miracles Magazine that she started several years ago. She collects true miracle stories for publication.
(Pages 98, 99, and 100)

Lilia Salazar, Ph.D., grew up in the Philippines, went to graduate school in Canada and immigrated to the US. She practices as a clinical psychologist in California, where she lives with her husband.
(Page 13)

Kathleen Ruckman is the published author of five children's books, articles, devotions, and poetry. She is currently writing devotionals on assignment for Guideposts Books, included in several collections. She resides in Central Oregon.
(Pages 34, 36, and 38)

Terri Picone reads and writes poems, stories, and someday soon will write a new blog post. When not reading or writing, she loves to cook new recipes, learn Italian, and tell her grandkids stories.

(Pages 32, 54, and 97)

Ava Pickard is an author, teacher, and Christian counselor in Texas. She has three grown children, four grandchildren who are her great joy. She is a widow and loves writing poetry, prose, and nonfiction inspirational books.

(Page 30)

Sue Miholer, a freelance editor (Picky, Picky Ink), also serves as the business manager of Oregon Christian Writers. She was a special education bus driver and classroom assistant around the turn of the century.

(Page 28)

Sandy McCulloch lives on a Washington coast canal where critters amaze and entertain. She is the author of "Canal Contemplations," a weekly blog to encourage others by connecting the everyday with God's grace and care.

(Page 96)

Maxine Marsolini is an author, life coach, and founder of Rebuilding Families. She finds dabbling in poetry is a great way to play with words for the sheer enjoyment of being creative. Most of her work is aimed at motivating others toward healthy relationships that honor each other and glorify the Lord.

(Pages 27 and 53)

Michael Mailloux started writing poems as a way to express his love of God. He hopes that people will come to know God and sense his joy for the Lord by reading his poems.

(Pages 93, 94, and 95)

Susan Thogerson Maas of Gresham, Oregon, loves wandering the woods with her camera. She writes devotionals and middle grade novels, which usually have some connection to God's beautiful creation.
(Page 92)

Rachel Lulich is a writer, editor, and Air Force veteran. When not exploring the world herself, Rachel creates worlds for others to enjoy. Her flagship project, the Fractured Galaxy series, is a near-future space adventure.
(Page 26)

Sherri Langton, associate editor of the *Bible Advocate* magazine and *Now What?*, has been published in *Focus on the Family*, *In Touch*, *Upper Room*, *Today's Christian Woman*, and other publications. She lives in Denver, Colorado.
(Page 12)

Grace Kyser is a retired professional who loves nature walks and sees God in them, often applying an analogy to life.
(Page 90)

Linda L. Kruschke writes candid memoir and fearless poetry. She blogs at AnotherFearlessYear.net and AnchoredVoices.com, and has poetry published in *Bible Advocate*, iBelieve.com, WeToo.org blog, and several anthologies. She is editor of *Swallow's Nest*.
(Pages 25, 87, and 88)

Julie Kepler lives in Banks, Oregon, with her husband of 22 years. She loves writing about our wonderful Creator and the beauty of His creation.
(Pages 84 and 85)

Yvonne Kays lives with her husband in the high desert of Central Oregon, and is a late bloomer to writing. Since retirement from teaching/prevention work in 2010, she writes stories and poems God puts on her heart.
(Pages 24 and 86)

Ginger Kauffman loves Jesus and she loves life. She writes about it on Salt & Pepper Blog: Life & Faith for Boomers & Beyond. You can find her at gingerkauffman.com.
(Pages 20, 22, and 52)

Charlotte Kardokus, of The Colony, Texas, is a wife, mother, and grandmother. A long-time OCW member and former newsletter editor, she is multi-published and was a finalist in the 2021 Cascade Christian Writers' Cascade Contest.
(Pages 18, 51, and 82)

Robin Illers has been writing poetry since she was in high school. Her first published poems were published in her father's Foreign Language Department's newsletter, written in French under a pseudonym. She has been published in *LIVE* and *The Standard*.
(Pages 15 and 16)

Sharon Chase Hoseley writes free verse and has authored *A Bridge Named Susan* and *Crossing the Bridge*. Sharon lives on the edge of Idaho, writes to relay God's blessings and walks through open doors.
(Page 71)

Tracie Heskett writes curriculum, leveled readers, teacher resource books, and Bible study materials. She has ghostwritten a couple of books and has had articles and poetry published.
(Page 50, 80, and 81)

Helen Heavirland, author, speaker, encourager, also teaches an online course, "Write Your Memories: Stories from Your Heart."
(Pages 78 and 79)

Retired, **Linda Heath** and husband Jerry live and travel in a 38-foot motorhome. Enjoying summers in Washington, they head south for the winter in Arizona. She recently discovered her tribe in the online writing community.
(Pages 49, 76, and 77)

Mary Hake has written poetry and stories since childhood. Written at 18, the poem here was after a snowy ride. Mary has been published in many periodicals and books and been in OCW 35 years.
(Page 74)

Debbie Goodwin has been writing and publishing for more than 40 years. She enjoyed connecting with OCW when she lived in Beaverton, Oregon. Now she lives in Roswell, Georgia, where she enjoys all things southern.
(Pages 14, 72, and 73)

As a podcaster and young adult writer, **Amy Earls** encourages teens to live by faith. Amy lives in Corvallis, Oregon, with one husband, two daughters, two guinea pigs, and a never-dying goldfish.
(Pages 46 and 69)

Chara Donahue is an adjunct professor at Corban University, co-author of multiple Experiencing Growth Bible studies, editor of AnchoredVoices.com, and host of the podcast The Bible Never Said That.
(Pages 45 and 70)

Dorothy Doede lives in Aloha, Oregon. She loves studying His story and writing about God's storytelling and creativity.
(Pages 10, 59, and 60)

Gail Denham's poetry, essays, newspaper articles, short stories and photos have been published nationally and internationally for more than 40 years. She has been a member of OCW since its beginning and taught many workshops at the conferences.
(Pages 48 and 68)

Shirley Dechaine lives in Tualatin, Oregon, with her husband and extended family. She especially enjoys spending time with her adult son, Paul, who has intellectual disabilities, and writing devotionals for his special needs friends.
(Page 64)

Laura Davis teaches piano in her home studio in Clackamas, Oregon. She treasures her faith, family and friends. A former English teacher, she also blogs, edits, proofreads and composes worship songs.
(Page 9)

Beryl Carpenter lives near the rain forest in Western Washington. She writes historical novels and poetry. She enjoys raking leaves and researching local history.
(Pages 8 and 62)

Susan Brehmer, host of the Encouraging Voice Podcast, believes treasure is found in the Word of God and time with Jesus sheds light on Scripture. Her original songs and Bible insights can be found at www.SusanBrehmer.com.
(Pages 5 and 44)

Tabitha B C Abel is now retired and more able to enjoy being a musician, athlete, and freelance Christian writer. Life still has challenges, but with her husband's support and a strong faith in God, nothing is insurmountable.

(Pages 6, 43, and 66)